AIR FRYER COOKBOOK 2022

EASY AND DELICIOUS RECIPES FOR BEGINNERS

SARAH SMITHSON

Table of Contents

Introduction 7
Air Fryer Lunch Recipes 10
Lentils Fritters 11
Lunch Potato Salad 13
Corn Casserole 15
Bacon and Garlic Pizzas 17
Sweet and Sour Sausage Mix 20
Meatballs and Tomato Sauce 22
Creamy Chicken Stew 33
Turkey Cakes 37
Cheese Ravioli and Marinara Sauce 40
Beef Stew 42
Meatballs Sandwich 44
Bacon Pudding 46
Special Lunch Seafood Stew 49
Air Fried Thai Salad 51
Zucchini Casserole 55
Coconut and Chicken Casserole 58
Turkey Burgers 60
Salmon and Asparagus 62
Easy Chicken Lunch 65
Chicken and Corn Casserole 66
Chicken and Zucchini Lunch Mix 68
Chicken, Beans, Corn and Quinoa Casserole 70
Air Fryer Side Dish Recipes 73
    Potato Wedges 73
Sweet Potato Fries 77
Corn with Lime and Cheese 79
Hasselback Potatoes 80
Brussels Sprouts Side Dish 82
Creamy Air Fried Potato Side Dish 84

Green Beans Side Dish	87
Roasted Pumpkin	88
Parmesan Mushrooms	90
Garlic Potatoes	92
Eggplant Side Dish	95
Mushrooms and Sour Cream	97
Eggplant Fries	99
Fried Tomatoes	101
Cauliflower Cakes	103
Creamy Brussels Sprouts	105
Cheddar Biscuits	108
Zucchini Fries	110
Roasted Peppers	112
Creamy Endives	114
Delicious Roasted Carrots	116
Vermouth Mushrooms	117
Roasted Parsnips	118
Barley Risotto	119
Glazed Beets	121
Beer Risotto	122
Cauliflower Rice	124
Carrots and Rhubarb	126
Roasted Eggplant	128
Delicious Air Fried Broccoli	130
Onion Rings Side Dish	131
Rice and Sausage Side Dish	133
Banana Chips	135
Spring Rolls	137
Crispy Radish Chips	139
Crab Sticks	141
Air Fried Dill Pickles	142
Chickpeas Snack	144
Sausage Balls	145
Chicken Dip	147
Sweet Popcorn	149
Apple Chips	151

Bread Sticks	152
Crispy Shrimp	154
Cajun Shrimp Appetizer	156
Crispy Fish Sticks	157
Fish Nuggets	159
Shrimp and Chestnut Rolls	161
Seafood Appetizer	163
Salmon Meatballs	165
Easy Chicken Wings	167
Chicken Breast Rolls	169
Crispy Chicken Breast Sticks	171
Beef Roll s	174
Empanadas	176
Greek Lamb Meatballs	178
Beef Party Rolls	179
Pork Rolls	182
Beef Patties	184
Roasted Bell Pepper Rolls	186
Stuffed Peppers	189
Olives Balls	192
Jalapeno Balls	194
Wrapped Shrimp	197
Broccoli Patties	199
Different Stuffed Peppers	201
Cheesy Zucchini Snack	203
Spinach Balls	205
Mushrooms Appetizer	207
Cheesy Party Wings	209
Cheese Sticks	211
Sweet Bacon Snack	213
Chicken Rolls	215
Conclusion	219

Introduction

Are you always looking for easier and more modern ways to cook the best meals for you and all your loved ones?
Are you constantly searching for useful kitchen appliances that will make your work in the kitchen more fun?
Well, you don't need to search anymore! We present to you today the best kitchen appliance available these days on the market: the air fryer!

Air fryers are simply the best kitchen tools for so many reasons. Are you interested in discovering more about air fryers? Then, pay attention next!

First of all, you need to know that air fryers are special and revolutionary kitchen appliances that cook your food using the circulation of hot air. These tools use a special technology called rapid air technology. Therefore, all the food you cook in these fryers is succulent on the inside and perfectly cooked on the outside.

The next thing you need to find out about air fryers is that they allow you to cook, bake, steam and roast pretty much everything you can imagine.

Last but not least, you should know that air fryers help you cook your meals in a much healthier way.
So many people all over the world just fell in love with this great and amazing tool and now it's your turn to become one of them.

So...long story short, we recommend you to purchase an air fryer right away and to get your hands on this cooking journal as soon as possible!

We can assure you that all the meals you cook in your air fryer will taste so good and that everyone will admire your cooking skills from now one!

So, let's get started!
Have fun cooking with your great air fryer!

Air Fryer Lunch Recipes

Lentils Fritters

Preparation time: 10 minutes **Cooking time:** 10 minutes
Servings: 2

Ingredients:

- 1 cup yellow lentils, soaked in water for 1 hour and drained
- 1 hot chili pepper, chopped
- 1 inch ginger piece, grated
- ½ teaspoon turmeric powder
- 1 teaspoon garam masala
- 1 teaspoon baking powder
- Salt and black pepper to the taste
- 2 teaspoons olive oil
- 1/3 cup water
- ½ cup cilantro, chopped
- 1 and ½ cup spinach, chopped
- 4 garlic cloves, minced
- ¾ cup red onion, chopped
- Mint chutney for serving

Directions:

1. In your blender, mix lentils with chili pepper, ginger, turmeric, garam masala, baking powder, salt, pepper, olive oil, water, cilantro, spinach, onion and garlic, blend well and shape medium balls out of this mix.
2. Place them all in your preheated air fryer at 400 degrees F and cook for 10 minutes.
3. Serve your veggie fritters with a side salad for lunch.

Enjoy!

Nutrition: calories 142, fat 2, fiber 8, carbs 12, protein 4

Lunch Potato Salad

Preparation time: 10 minutes **Cooking time:** 25 minutes
Servings: 4

Ingredients:

- 2 pound red potatoes, halved
- 2 tablespoons olive oil
- Salt and black pepper to the taste
- 2 green onions, chopped
- 1 red bell pepper, chopped
- 1/3 cup lemon juice
- 3 tablespoons mustard

Directions:

1. On your air fryer's basket, mix potatoes with half of the olive oil, salt and pepper and cook at 350 degrees F for 25 minutes shaking the fryer once.
2. In a bowl, mix onions with bell pepper and roasted potatoes and toss.

3. In a small bowl, mix lemon juice with the rest of the oil and mustard and whisk really well.
4. Add this to potato salad, toss well and serve for lunch. Enjoy!

Nutrition: calories 211, fat 6, fiber 8, carbs 12, protein 4

Corn Casserole

Preparation time: 10 minutes **Cooking time:** 15 minutes
Servings: 4

Ingredients:
- 2 cups corn
- 3 tablespoons flour
- 1 egg
- ¼ cup milk
- ½ cup light cream
- ½ cup Swiss cheese, grated
- 2 tablespoons butter
- Salt and black pepper to the taste
- Cooking spray

Directions:
1. In a bowl, mix corn with flour, egg, milk, light cream, cheese, salt, pepper and butter and stir well.
2. Grease your air fryer's pan with cooking spray, pour cream mix, spread and cook at 320 degrees F for 15 minutes.
3. Serve warm for lunch.

Enjoy!

Nutrition: calories 281, fat 7, fiber 8, carbs 9, protein 6

Bacon and Garlic Pizzas

Preparation time: 10 minutes **Cooking time:** 10 minutes
Servings: 4

Ingredients:

- 4 dinner rolls, frozen
- 4 garlic cloves minced
- ½ teaspoon oregano dried
- ½ teaspoon garlic powder
- 1 cup tomato sauce
- 8 bacon slices, cooked and chopped
- 1 and ¼ cups cheddar cheese, grated
- Cooking spray

Directions:

1. Place dinner rolls on a working surface and press them to obtain 4 ovals.
2. Spray each oval with cooking spray, transfer them to your air fryer and cook them at 370 degrees F for 2 minutes.

3. Spread tomato sauce on each oval, divide garlic, sprinkle oregano and garlic powder and top with bacon and cheese.
4. Return pizzas to your heated air fryer and cook them at 370 degrees F for 8 minutes more.
5. Serve them warm for lunch.

Enjoy!

Nutrition: calories 217, fat 5, fiber 8, carbs 12, protein 4

Sweet and Sour Sausage Mix

Preparation time: 10 minutes **Cooking time:** 10 minutes
Servings: 4

Ingredients:

- 1 pound sausages, sliced
- 1 red bell pepper, cut into strips
- ½ cup yellow onion, chopped
- 3 tablespoons brown sugar
- 1/3 cup ketchup
- 2 tablespoons mustard
- 2 tablespoons apple cider vinegar
- ½ cup chicken stock

Directions:
1. In a bowl, mix sugar with ketchup, mustard, stock and vinegar and whisk well.
2. In your air fryer's pan, mix sausage slices with bell pepper, onion and sweet and sour mix, toss and cook at 350 degrees F for 10 minutes.
3. Divide into bowls and serve for lunch.

Enjoy!

Nutrition: calories 162, fat 6, fiber 9, carbs 12, protein 6

Meatballs and Tomato Sauce

Preparation time: 10 minutes **Cooking time:** 15 minutes
Servings: 4

Ingredients:

- 1 pound lean beef, ground
- 3 green onions, chopped
- 2 garlic cloves, minced
- 1 egg yolk
- ¼ cup bread crumbs
- Salt and black pepper to the taste
- 1 tablespoon olive oil
- 16 ounces tomato sauce
- 2 tablespoons mustard

Directions:

1. In a bowl, mix beef with onion, garlic, egg yolk, bread crumbs, salt and pepper, stir well and shape medium meatballs out of this mix.
2. Grease meatballs with the oil, place them in your air fryer and cook them at 400 degrees F for 10 minutes.

3. In a bowl, mix tomato sauce with mustard, whisk, add over meatballs, toss them and cook at 400 degrees F for 5 minutes more.
4. Divide meatballs and sauce on plates and serve for lunch.

Enjoy!

Nutrition: calories 300, fat 8, fiber 9, carbs 16, protein 5

Stuffed Meatballs

Preparation time: 10 minutes **Cooking time:** 10 minutes
Servings: 4

Ingredients:
- 1/3 cup bread crumbs
- 3 tablespoons milk
- 1 tablespoon ketchup
- 1 egg
- ½ teaspoon marjoram, dried
- Salt and black pepper to the taste
- 1 pound lean beef, ground
- 20 cheddar cheese cubes
- 1 tablespoon olive oil

Directions:
1. In a bowl, mix bread crumbs with ketchup, milk, marjoram, salt, pepper and egg and whisk well.
2. Add beef, stir and shape 20 meatballs out of this mix.
3. Shape each meatball around a cheese cube, drizzle the oil over them and rub.
4. Place all meatballs in your preheated air fryer and cook at 390 degrees F for 10 minutes.
5. Serve them for lunch with a side salad.

Enjoy!

Nutrition: calories 200, fat 5, fiber 8, carbs 12, protein 5

Steaks and Cabbage

Preparation time: 10 minutes **Cooking time:** 10 minutes

Servings: 4

Ingredients:

- ½ pound sirloin steak, cut into strips
- 2 teaspoons cornstarch
- 1 tablespoon peanut oil
- 2 cups green cabbage, chopped
- 1 yellow bell pepper, chopped
- 2 green onions, chopped
- 2 garlic cloves, minced
- Salt and black pepper to the taste

Directions:

1. In a bowl, mix cabbage with salt, pepper and peanut oil, toss, transfer to air fryer's basket, cook at 370 degrees F for 4 minutes and transfer to a bowl.
2. Add steak strips to your air fryer, also add green onions, bell pepper, garlic, salt and pepper, toss and cook for 5 minutes.
3. Add over cabbage, toss, divide among plates and serve for lunch.

Enjoy!

Nutrition: calories 282, fat 6, fiber 8, carbs 14, protein 6

Succulent Lunch Turkey Breast

Preparation time: 10 minutes **Cooking time:** 47 minutes
Servings: 4

Ingredients:

- 1 big turkey breast
- 2 teaspoons olive oil
- ½ teaspoon smoked paprika
- 1 teaspoon thyme, dried
- ½ teaspoon sage, dried
- Salt and black pepper to the taste
- 2 tablespoons mustard
- ¼ cup maple syrup
- 1 tablespoon butter, soft

Directions:

1. Brush turkey breast with the olive oil, season with salt, pepper, thyme, paprika and sage, rub, place in your air fryer's basket and fry at 350 degrees F for 25 minutes.
2. Flip turkey, cook for 10 minutes more, flip one more time and cook for another 10 minutes.

3. Meanwhile, heat up a pan with the butter over medium heat, add mustard and maple syrup, stir well, cook for a couple of minutes and take off heat.
4. Slice turkey breast, divide among plates and serve with the maple glaze drizzled on top.

Enjoy!

Nutrition: calories 280, fat 2, fiber 7, carbs 16, protein 14

Italian Eggplant Sandwich

Preparation time: 10 minutes **Cooking time:** 16 minutes
Servings: 2

Ingredients:

- 1 eggplant, sliced
- 2 teaspoons parsley, dried
- Salt and black pepper to the taste
- ½ cup breadcrumbs
- ½ teaspoon Italian seasoning
- ½ teaspoon garlic powder
- ½ teaspoon onion powder
- 2 tablespoons milk
- 4 bread slices
- Cooking spray
- ½ cup mayonnaise
- ¾ cup tomato sauce
- 2 cups mozzarella cheese, grated

Directions:

1. Season eggplant slices with salt and pepper, leave aside for 10 minutes and then pat dry them well.

2. In a bowl, mix parsley with breadcrumbs, Italian seasoning, onion and garlic powder, salt and black pepper and stir.
3. In another bowl, mix milk with mayo and whisk well.
4. Brush eggplant slices with mayo mix, dip them in breadcrumbs, place them in your air fryer's basket, spray with cooking oil and cook them at 400 degrees F for 15 minutes, flipping them after 8 minutes.
5. Brush each bread slice with olive oil and arrange 2 on a working surface.
6. Add mozzarella and parmesan on each, add baked eggplant slices, spread tomato sauce and basil and top with the other bread slices, greased side down.
7. Divide sandwiches on plates, cut them in halves and serve for lunch.

Enjoy!

Nutrition: calories 324, fat 16, fiber 4, carbs 39, protein 12

Creamy Chicken Stew

Preparation time: 10 minutes **Cooking time:** 25 minutes
Servings: 4

Ingredients:

- 1 and ½ cups canned cream of celery soup
- 6 chicken tenders
- Salt and black pepper to the taste
- 2 potatoes, chopped
- 1 bay leaf
- 1 thyme spring, chopped
- 1 tablespoon milk
- 1 egg yolk
- ½ cup heavy cream

Directions:
1. In a bowl, mix chicken with cream of celery, potatoes, heavy cream, bay leaf, thyme, salt and pepper, toss, pour into your air fryer's pan and cook at 320 degrees F for 25 minutes.
2. Leave your stew to cool down a bit, discard bay leaf, divide among plates and serve right away.

Enjoy!

Nutrition: calories 300, fat 11, fiber 2, carbs 23, protein 14

Lunch Pork and Potatoes

Preparation time: 10 minutes **Cooking time:** 25 minutes
Servings: 2

Ingredients:
- 2 pounds pork loin
- Salt and black pepper to the taste
- 2 red potatoes, cut into medium wedges
- ½ teaspoon garlic powder
- ½ teaspoon red pepper flakes
- 1 teaspoon parsley, dried
- A drizzle of balsamic vinegar

Directions:
1. In your air fryer's pan, mix pork with potatoes, salt, pepper, garlic powder, pepper flakes, parsley and vinegar, toss and cook at 390 degrees F for 25 minutes.
2. Slice pork, divide it and potatoes on plates and serve for lunch.

Enjoy!

Nutrition: calories 400, fat 15, fiber 7, carbs 27, protein 20

Turkey Cakes

Preparation time: 10 minutes **Cooking time:** 10 minutes
Servings: 4

Ingredients:
- 6 mushrooms, chopped
- 1 teaspoon garlic powder
- 1 teaspoon onion powder
- Salt and black pepper to the taste
- 1 and ¼ pounds turkey meat, ground
- Cooking spray
- Tomato sauce for serving

Directions:
1. In your blender, mix mushrooms with salt and pepper, pulse well and transfer to a bowl.
2. Add turkey, onion powder, garlic powder, salt and pepper, stir and shape cakes out of this mix.
3. Spray them with cooking spray, transfer them to your air fryer and cook at 320 degrees F for 10 minutes.
4. Serve them with tomato sauce on the side and a tasty side salad.

Enjoy!

Nutrition: calories 202, fat 6, fiber 3, carbs 17, protein 10

Cheese Ravioli and Marinara Sauce

Preparation time: 10 minutes **Cooking time:** 8 minutes
Servings: 6

Ingredients:

- 20 ounces cheese ravioli
- 10 ounces marinara sauce
- 1 tablespoon olive oil
- 1 cup buttermilk
- 2 cups bread crumbs
- ¼ cup parmesan, grated

Directions:
1. Put buttermilk in a bowl and breadcrumbs in another bowl.
2. Dip ravioli in buttermilk, then in breadcrumbs and place them in your air fryer on a baking sheet.
3. Drizzle olive oil over them, cook at 400 degrees F for 5 minutes, divide them on plates, sprinkle parmesan on top and serve for lunch

Enjoy!

Nutrition: calories 270, fat 12, fiber 6, carbs 30, protein 15

Beef Stew

Preparation time: 10 minutes **Cooking time:** 20 minutes
Servings: 4

Ingredients:
- 2 pounds beef meat, cut into medium chunks
- 2 carrots, chopped
- 4 potatoes, chopped
- Salt and black pepper to the taste
- 1 quart veggie stock
- ½ teaspoon smoked paprika
- A handful thyme, chopped

Directions:
1. In a dish that fits your air fryer, mix beef with carrots, potatoes, stock, salt, pepper, paprika and thyme, stir, place in air fryer's basket and cook at 375 degrees F for 20 minutes.
2. Divide into bowls and serve right away for lunch.

Enjoy!

Nutrition: calories 260, fat 5, fiber 8, carbs 20, protein 22

Meatballs Sandwich

Preparation time: 10 minutes **Cooking time:** 22 minutes
Servings: 4

Ingredients:

- 3 baguettes, sliced more than halfway through
- 14 ounces beef, ground
- 7 ounces tomato sauce
- 1 small onion, chopped
- 1 egg, whisked
- 1 tablespoon bread crumbs
- 2 tablespoons cheddar cheese, grated
- 1 tablespoon oregano, chopped
- 1 tablespoon olive oil
- Salt and black pepper to the taste
- 1 teaspoon thyme, dried
- 1 teaspoon basil, dried

Directions:

1. In a bowl, combine meat with salt, pepper, onion, breadcrumbs, egg, cheese, oregano, thyme and basil,

stir, shape medium meatballs and add them to your air fryer after you've greased it with the oil.
2. Cook them at 375 degrees F for 12 minutes, flipping them halfway.
3. Add tomato sauce, cook meatballs for 10 minutes more and arrange them on sliced baguettes.
4. Serve them right away.

Enjoy!

Nutrition: calories 380, fat 5, fiber 6, carbs 34, protein 20

Bacon Pudding

Preparation time: 10 minutes **Cooking time:** 30 minutes
Servings: 6

Ingredients:

- 4 bacon strips, cooked and chopped
- 1 tablespoon butter, soft
- 2 cups corn
- 1 yellow onion, chopped
- ¼ cup celery, chopped
- ½ cup red bell pepper, chopped
- 1 teaspoon thyme, chopped
- 2 teaspoons garlic, minced
- Salt and black pepper to the taste
- ½ cup heavy cream
- 1 and ½ cups milk
- 3 eggs, whisked
- 3 cups bread, cubed
- 4 tablespoons parmesan, grated
- Cooking spray

Directions:

1. Grease your air fryer's pan with coking spray.
2. In a bowl, mix bacon with butter, corn, onion, bell pepper, celery, thyme, garlic, salt, pepper, milk, heavy cream, eggs and bread cubes, toss, pour into greased pan and sprinkle cheese all over
3. Add this to your preheated air fryer at 320 degrees and cook for 30 minutes.
4. Divide among plates and serve warm for a quick lunch.

Enjoy!

Nutrition: calories 276, fat 10, fiber 2, carbs 20, protein 10

Special Lunch Seafood Stew

Preparation time: 10 minutes **Cooking time:** 20 minutes
Servings: 4

Ingredients:

- 5 ounces white rice
- 2 ounces peas
- 1 red bell pepper, chopped
- 14 ounces white wine
- 3 ounces water
- 2 ounces squid pieces
- 7 ounces mussels
- 3 ounces sea bass fillet, skinless, boneless and chopped
- 6 scallops
- 3.5 ounces clams
- 4 shrimp
- 4 crayfish
- Salt and black pepper to the taste
- 1 tablespoon olive oil

Directions:

1. In your air fryer's pan, mix sea bass with shrimp, mussels, scallops, crayfish, clams and squid.
2. Add the oil, salt and pepper and toss to coat.
3. In a bowl, mix peas salt, pepper, bell pepper and rice and stir.
4. Add this over seafood, also add whine and water, place pan in your air fryer and cook at 400 degrees F for 20 minutes, stirring halfway.
5. Divide into bowls and serve for lunch.

Enjoy!

Nutrition: calories 300, fat 12, fiber 2, carbs 23, protein 25

Air Fried Thai Salad

Preparation time: 10 minutes **Cooking time:** 5 minutes
Servings: 4

Ingredients:
- 1 cup carrots, grated
- 1 cup red cabbage, shredded
- A pinch of salt and black pepper
- A handful cilantro, chopped
- 1 small cucumber, chopped
- Juice from 1 lime
- 2 teaspoons red curry paste
- 12 big shrimp, cooked, peeled and deveined

Directions:
1. In a pan that fits your, mix cabbage with carrots, cucumber and shrimp, toss, introduce in your air fryer and cook at 360 degrees F for 5 minutes.
2. Add salt, pepper, cilantro, lime juice and red curry paste, toss again, divide among plates and serve right away.

Enjoy!

Nutrition: calories 172, fat 5, fiber 7, carbs 8, protein 5

Sweet Potato Lunch Casserole

Preparation time: 10 minutes **Cooking time:** 50 minutes
Servings: 6

Ingredients:
- 3 big sweet potatoes, pricked with a fork
- 1 cup chicken stock
- Salt and black pepper to the taste
- A pinch of cayenne pepper
- ¼ teaspoon nutmeg, ground
- 1/3 cup coconut cream

Directions:
1. Place sweet potatoes in your air fryer, cook them at 350 degrees F for 40 minutes, cool them down, peel, roughly chop and transfer to a pan that fits your air fryer.
2. Add stock, salt, pepper, cayenne and coconut cream, toss, introduce in your air fryer and cook at 360 degrees F for 10 minutes more.
3. Divide casserole into bowls and serve.

Enjoy!

Nutrition: calories 245, fat 4, fiber 5, carbs 10, protein 6

Zucchini Casserole

Preparation time: 10 minutes **Cooking time:** 16 minutes
Servings: 8

Ingredients:

- 1 cup veggie stock
- 2 tablespoons olive oil
- 2 sweet potatoes, peeled and cut into medium wedges
- 8 zucchinis, cut into medium wedges
- 2 yellow onions, chopped
- 1 cup coconut milk
- Salt and black pepper to the taste
- 1 tablespoon soy sauce
- ¼ teaspoon thyme, dried
- ¼ teaspoon rosemary, dried
- 4 tablespoons dill, chopped
- ½ teaspoon basil, chopped

Directions:

1. Heat up a pan that fits your air fryer with the oil over medium heat, add onion, stir and cook for 2 minutes.

2. Add zucchinis, thyme, rosemary, basil, potato, salt, pepper, stock, milk, soy sauce and dill, stir, introduce in your air fryer, cook at 360 degrees F for 14 minutes, divide among plates and serve right away.

Enjoy!

Nutrition: calories 133, fat 3, fiber 4, carbs 10, protein 5

Coconut and Chicken Casserole

Preparation time: 10 minutes **Cooking time:** 25 minutes
Servings: 4

Ingredients:

- 4 lime leaves, torn
- 1 cup veggie stock
- 1 lemongrass stalk, chopped
- 1 inch piece, grated
- 1 pound chicken breast, skinless, boneless and cut into thin strips
- 8 ounces mushrooms, chopped
- 4 Thai chilies, chopped
- 4 tablespoons fish sauce
- 6 ounces coconut milk
- ¼ cup lime juice
- ¼ cup cilantro, chopped
- Salt and black pepper to the taste

Directions:

1. Put stock into a pan that fits your air fryer, bring to a simmer over medium heat, add lemongrass, ginger and lime leaves, stir and cook for 10 minutes.
2. Strain soup, return to pan, add chicken, mushrooms, milk, chilies, fish sauce, lime juice, cilantro, salt and pepper, stir, introduce in your air fryer and cook at 360 degrees F for 15 minutes.
3. Divide into bowls and serve.

Enjoy!

Nutrition: calories 150, fat 4, fiber 4, carbs 6, protein 7

Turkey Burgers

Preparation time: 10 minutes **Cooking time:** 8 minutes
Servings: 4

Ingredients:
- 1 pound turkey meat, ground
- 1 shallot, minced
- A drizzle of olive oil
- 1 small jalapeno pepper, minced
- 2 teaspoons lime juice
- Zest from 1 lime, grated
- Salt and black pepper to the taste
- 1 teaspoon cumin, ground
- 1 teaspoon sweet paprika
- Guacamole for serving

Directions:

1. In a bowl, mix turkey meat with salt, pepper, cumin, paprika, shallot, jalapeno, lime juice and zest, stir well, shape burgers from this mix, drizzle the oil over them, introduce in preheated air fryer and cook them at 370 degrees F for 8 minutes on each side.
2. Divide among plates and serve with guacamole on top. Enjoy!

Nutrition: calories 200, fat 12, fiber 0, carbs 0, protein 12

Salmon and Asparagus

Preparation time: 10 minutes **Cooking time:** 23 minutes
Servings: 4

Ingredients:
- 1 pound asparagus, trimmed
- 1 tablespoon olive oil
- A pinch of sweet paprika
- Salt and black pepper to the taste
- A pinch of garlic powder
- A pinch of cayenne pepper
- 1 red bell pepper, cut into halves
- 4 ounces smoked salmon

Directions:
1. Put asparagus spears and bell pepper on a lined baking sheet that fits your air fryer, add salt, pepper, garlic powder, paprika, olive oil, cayenne pepper, toss to coat, introduce in the fryer, cook at 390 degrees F for 8 minutes, flip and cook for 8 minutes more.
2. Add salmon, cook for 5 minutes, more, divide everything on plates and serve.

Enjoy!

Nutrition: calories 90, fat 1, fiber 1, carbs 1.2, protein 4

Easy Chicken Lunch

Preparation time: 10 minutes **Cooking time:** 20 minutes
Servings: 6

Ingredients:
- 1 bunch kale, chopped
- Salt and black pepper to the taste
- ¼ cup chicken stock
- 1 cup chicken, shredded
- 3 carrots, chopped
- 1 cup shiitake mushrooms, roughly sliced

Directions:
1. In a blender, mix stock with kale, pulse a few times and pour into a pan that fits your air fryer.
2. Add chicken, mushrooms, carrots, salt and pepper to the taste, toss, introduce in your air fryer and cook at 350 degrees F for 18 minutes.

Enjoy!

Nutrition: calories 180, fat 7, fiber 2, carbs 10, protein 5

Chicken and Corn Casserole

Preparation time: 10 minutes **Cooking time:** 30 minutes
Servings: 6

Ingredients:

- 1 cup clean chicken stock
- 2 teaspoons garlic powder
- Salt and black pepper to the taste
- 6 ounces canned coconut milk
- 1 and ½ cups green lentils
- 2 pounds chicken breasts, skinless, boneless and cubed
- 1/3 cup cilantro, chopped
- 3 cups corn
- 3 handfuls spinach
- 3 green onions, chopped

Directions:

1. In a pan that fits your air fryer, mix stock with coconut milk, salt, pepper, garlic powder, chicken and lentils.

2. Add corn, green onions, cilantro and spinach, stir well, introduce in your air fryer and cook at 350 degrees F for 30 minutes.

Enjoy!

Nutrition: calories 345, fat 12, fiber 10, carbs 20, protein 44

Chicken and Zucchini Lunch Mix

Preparation time: 10 minutes **Cooking time:** 20 minutes
Servings: 4

Ingredients:

- 4 zucchinis, cut with a spiralizer
- 1 pound chicken breasts, skinless, boneless and cubed
- 2 garlic cloves, minced
- 1 teaspoon olive oil
- Salt and black pepper to the taste
- 2 cups cherry tomatoes, halved
- ½ cup almonds, chopped

For the pesto:

- 2 cups basil
- 2 cups kale, chopped
- 1 tablespoon lemon juice
- 1 garlic clove
- ¾ cup pine nuts
- ½ cup olive oil
- A pinch of salt

Directions:
1. In your food processor, mix basil with kale, lemon juice, garlic, pine nuts, oil and a pinch of salt, pulse really well and leave aside.
2. Heat up a pan that fits your air fryer with the oil over medium heat, add garlic, stir and cook for 1 minute.
3. Add chicken, salt, pepper, stir, almonds, zucchini noodles, garlic, cherry tomatoes and the pesto you've made at the beginning, stir gently, introduce in preheated air fryer and cook at 360 degrees F for 17 minutes.
4. Divide among plates and serve for lunch.

Enjoy!

Nutrition: calories 344, fat 8, fiber 7, carbs 12, protein 16

Chicken, Beans, Corn and Quinoa Casserole

Preparation time: 10 minutes **Cooking time:** 30 minutes
Servings: 8

Ingredients:

- 1 cup quinoa, already cooked
- 3 cups chicken breast, cooked and shredded
- 14 ounces canned black beans
- 12 ounces corn
- ½ cup cilantro, chopped
- 6 kale leaves, chopped
- ½ cup green onions, chopped
- 1 cup clean tomato sauce
- 1 cup clean salsa
- 2 teaspoons chili powder
- 2 teaspoons cumin, ground
- 3 cups mozzarella cheese, shredded
- 1 tablespoon garlic powder
- Cooking spray
- 2 jalapeno peppers, chopped

Directions:

1. Spray a baking dish that fits your air fryer with cooking spray, add quinoa, chicken, black beans, corn, cilantro, kale, green onions, tomato sauce, salsa, chili powder, cumin, garlic powder, jalapenos and mozzarella, toss, introduce in your fryer and cook at 350 degrees F for 17 minutes.
2. Slice and serve warm for lunch.

Enjoy!

Nutrition: calories 365, fat 12, fiber 6, carbs 22, protein 26

Air Fryer Side Dish Recipes

Potato Wedges

Preparation time: 10 minutes **Cooking time:** 25 minutes
Servings: 4

Ingredients:

- 2 potatoes, cut into wedges
- 1 tablespoon olive oil
- Salt and black pepper to the taste
- 3 tablespoons sour cream
- 2 tablespoons sweet chili sauce

Directions:
1. In a bowl, mix potato wedges with oil, salt and pepper, toss well, add to air fryer's basket and cook at 360 degrees F for 25 minutes, flipping them once.
2. Divide potato wedges on plates, drizzle sour cream and chili sauce all over and serve them as a side dish.

Enjoy!

Nutrition: calories 171, fat 8, fiber 9, carbs 18, protein 7

Mushroom Side Dish

Preparation time: 10 minutes **Cooking time:** 8 minutes
Servings: 4

Ingredients:

- 10 button mushrooms, stems removed
- 1 tablespoon Italian seasoning
- Salt and black pepper to the taste
- 2 tablespoons cheddar cheese, grated
- 1 tablespoon olive oil
- 2 tablespoons mozzarella, grated
- 1 tablespoon dill, chopped

Directions:
1. In a bowl, mix mushrooms with Italian seasoning, salt, pepper, oil and dill and rub well.
2. Arrange mushrooms in your air fryer's basket, sprinkle mozzarella and cheddar in each and cook them at 360 degrees F for 8 minutes.
3. Divide them on plates and serve them as a side dish.

Enjoy!

Nutrition: calories 241, fat 7, fiber 8, carbs 14, protein 6

Sweet Potato Fries

Preparation time: 10 minutes **Cooking time:** 20 minutes
Servings: 2

Ingredients:

- 2 sweet potatoes, peeled and cut into medium fries
- Salt and black pepper to the taste
- 2 tablespoons olive oil
- ½ teaspoon curry powder
- ¼ teaspoon coriander, ground
- ¼ cup ketchup
- 2 tablespoons mayonnaise
- ½ teaspoon cumin, ground
- A pinch of ginger powder
- A pinch of cinnamon powder

Directions:

1. In your air fryer's basket, mix sweet potato fries with salt, pepper, coriander, curry powder and oil, toss well and cook at 370 degrees F for 20 minutes, flipping them once.

2. Meanwhile, in a bowl, mix ketchup with mayo, cumin, ginger and cinnamon and whisk well.
3. Divide fries on plates, drizzle ketchup mix over them and serve as a side dish.

Enjoy!

Nutrition: calories 200, fat 5, fiber 8, carbs 9, protein 7

Corn with Lime and Cheese

Preparation time: 10 minutes **Cooking time:** 15 minutes
Servings: 2

Ingredients:
- 2 corns on the cob, husks removed
- A drizzle of olive oil
- ½ cup feta cheese, grated
- 2 teaspoons sweet paprika
- Juice from 2 limes

Directions:
1. Rub corn with oil and paprika, place in your air fryer and cook at 400 degrees F for 15 minutes, flipping once.
2. Divide corn on plates, sprinkle cheese on top, drizzle lime juice and serve as a side dish.

Enjoy!

Nutrition: calories 200, fat 5, fiber 2, carbs 6, protein 6

Hasselback Potatoes

Preparation time: 10 minutes **Cooking time:** 20 minutes
Servings: 2

Ingredients:

- 2 potatoes, peeled and thinly sliced almost all the way horizontally
- 2 tablespoons olive oil
- 1 teaspoon garlic, minced
- Salt and black pepper to the taste
- ½ teaspoon oregano, dried
- ½ teaspoon basil, dried
- ½ teaspoon sweet paprika

Directions:
1. In a bowl, mix oil with garlic, salt, pepper, oregano, basil and paprika and whisk really well.
2. Rub potatoes with this mix, place them in your air fryer's basket and fry them at 360 degrees F for 20 minutes.
3. Divide them on plates and serve as a side dish.

Enjoy!

Nutrition: calories 172, fat 6, fiber 6, carbs 9, protein 6

Brussels Sprouts Side Dish

Preparation time: 10 minutes **Cooking time:** 15 minutes
Servings: 4

Ingredients:

- 1 pound Brussels sprouts, trimmed and halved
- Salt and black pepper to the taste
- 6 teaspoons olive oil
- ½ teaspoon thyme, chopped
- ½ cup mayonnaise
- 2 tablespoons roasted garlic, crushed

Directions:
1. In your air fryer, mix Brussels sprouts with salt, pepper and oil, toss well and cook them at 390 degrees F for 15 minutes.
2. Meanwhile, in a bowl, mix thyme with mayo and garlic and whisk well.
3. Divide Brussels sprouts on plates, drizzle garlic sauce all over and serve as a side dish.

Enjoy!

Nutrition: calories 172, fat 6, fiber 8, carbs 12, protein 6

Creamy Air Fried Potato Side Dish

Preparation time: 10 minutes **Cooking time:** 1 hour and 20 minutes **Servings:** 2

Ingredients:

- 1 big potato
- 2 bacon strips, cooked and chopped
- 1 teaspoon olive oil
- 1/3 cup cheddar cheese, shredded
- 1 tablespoon green onions, chopped
- Salt and black pepper to the taste
- 1 tablespoon butter
- 2 tablespoons heavy cream

Directions:

1. Rub potato with oil, season with salt and pepper, place in preheated air fryer and cook at 400 degrees F for 30 minutes.
2. Flip potato, cook for 30 minutes more, transfer to a cutting board, cool it down, slice in half lengthwise and scoop pulp in a bowl.

3. Add bacon, cheese, butter, heavy cream, green onions, salt and pepper, stir well and stuff potato skins with this mix.
4. Return potatoes to your air fryer and cook them at 400 degrees F for 20 minutes.
5. Divide among plates and serve as a side dish.

Enjoy!

Nutrition: calories 172, fat 5, fiber 7, carbs 9, protein 4

Green Beans Side Dish

Preparation time: 10 minutes **Cooking time:** 25 minutes
Servings: 4

Ingredients:

- 1 and ½ pounds green beans, trimmed and steamed for 2 minutes
- Salt and black pepper to the taste
- ½ pound shallots, chopped
- ¼ cup almonds, toasted
- 2 tablespoons olive oil

Directions:

1. In your air fryer's basket, mix green beans with salt, pepper, shallots, almonds and oil, toss well and cook at 400 degrees F for 25 minutes.
2. Divide among plates and serve as a side dish.

Enjoy!

Nutrition: calories 152, fat 3, fiber 6, carbs 7, protein 4

Roasted Pumpkin

Preparation time: 10 minutes **Cooking time:** 12 minutes
Servings: 4

Ingredients:

- 1 and ½ pound pumpkin, deseeded, sliced and roughly chopped
- 3 garlic cloves, minced
- 1 tablespoon olive oil
- A pinch of sea salt
- A pinch of brown sugar
- A pinch of nutmeg, ground
- A pinch of cinnamon powder

Directions:
1. In your air fryer's basket, mix pumpkin with garlic, oil, salt, brown sugar, cinnamon and nutmeg, toss well, cover and cook at 370 degrees F for 12 minutes.
2. Divide among plates and serve as a side dish.

Enjoy!

Nutrition: calories 200, fat 5, fiber 4, carbs 7, protein 4

Parmesan Mushrooms

Preparation time: 10 minutes **Cooking time:** 15 minutes
Servings: 3

Ingredients:
- 9 button mushroom caps
- 3 cream cracker slices, crumbled
- 1 egg white
- 2 tablespoons parmesan, grated
- 1 teaspoon Italian seasoning
- A pinch of salt and black pepper
- 1 tablespoon butter, melted

Directions:

1. In a bowl, mix crackers with egg white, parmesan, Italian seasoning, butter, salt and pepper, stir well and stuff mushrooms with this mix.
2. Arrange mushrooms in your air fryer's basket and cook them at 360 degrees F for 15 minutes.
3. Divide among plates and serve as a side dish.

Enjoy!

Nutrition: calories 124, fat 4, fiber 4, carbs 7, protein 3

Garlic Potatoes

Preparation time: 10 minutes **Cooking time:** 20 minutes
Servings: 6

Ingredients:

- 2 tablespoons parsley, chopped
- 5 garlic cloves, minced
- ½ teaspoon basil, dried
- ½ teaspoon oregano, dried
- 3 pounds red potatoes, halved
- 1 teaspoon thyme, dried
- 2 tablespoons olive oil
- Salt and black pepper to the taste
- 2 tablespoons butter
- 1/3 cup parmesan, grated

Directions:

1. In a bowl, mix potato halves with parsley, garlic, basil, oregano, thyme, salt, pepper, oil and butter, toss really well and transfer to your air fryer's basket.
2. Cover and cook at 400 degrees F for 20 minutes, flipping them once.
3. Sprinkle parmesan on top, divide potatoes on plates and serve as a side dish.

Enjoy!

Nutrition: calories 162, fat 5, fiber 5, carbs 7, protein 5

Eggplant Side Dish

Preparation time: 10 minutes **Cooking time:** 10 minutes
Servings: 4

Ingredients:

- 8 baby eggplants, scooped in the center and pulp reserved
- Salt and black pepper to the taste
- A pinch of oregano, dried
- 1 green bell pepper, chopped
- 1 tablespoon tomato paste
- 1 bunch coriander, chopped
- ½ teaspoon garlic powder
- 1 tablespoon olive oil
- 1 yellow onion, chopped
- 1 tomato chopped

Directions:

1. Heat up a pan with the oil over medium heat, add onion, stir and cook for 1 minute.
2. Add salt, pepper, eggplant pulp, oregano, green bell pepper, tomato paste, garlic power, coriander and

tomato, stir, cook for 1-2 minutes more, take off heat and cool down.
3. Stuff eggplants with this mix, place them in your air fryer's basket and cook at 360 degrees F for 8 minutes.
4. Divide eggplants on plates and serve them as a side dish.

Enjoy!

Nutrition: calories 200, fat 3, fiber 7, carbs 12, protein 4

Mushrooms and Sour Cream

Preparation time: 10 minutes **Cooking time:** 10 minutes
Servings: 6

Ingredients:
- 2 bacon strips, chopped
- 1 yellow onion, chopped
- 1 green bell pepper, chopped
- 24 mushrooms, stems removed
- 1 carrot, grated
- ½ cup sour cream
- 1 cup cheddar cheese, grated
- Salt and black pepper to the taste

Directions:
1. Heat up a pan over medium high heat, add bacon, onion, bell pepper and carrot, stir and cook for 1 minute.
2. Add salt, pepper and sour cream, stir cook for 1 minute more, take off heat and cool down.
3. Stuff mushrooms with this mix, sprinkle cheese on top and cook at 360 degrees F for 8 minutes.
4. Divide among plates and serve as a side dish.

Enjoy!

Nutrition: calories 211, fat 4, fiber 7, carbs 8, protein 3

Eggplant Fries

Preparation time: 10 minutes **Cooking time:** 5 minutes
Servings: 4

Ingredients:

- Cooking spray
- 1 eggplant, peeled and cut into medium fries
- 2 tablespoons milk
- 1 egg, whisked
- 2 cups panko bread crumbs
- ½ cup Italian cheese, shredded
- A pinch of salt and black pepper to the taste

Directions:
1. In a bowl, mix egg with milk, salt and pepper and whisk well.
2. In another bowl, mix panko with cheese and stir.
3. Dip eggplant fries in egg mix, then coat in panko mix, place them in your air fryer greased with cooking spray and cook at 400 degrees F for 5 minutes.
4. Divide among plates and serve as a side dish.

Enjoy!

Nutrition: calories 162, fat 5, fiber 5, carbs 7, protein 6

Fried Tomatoes

Preparation time: 10 minutes **Cooking time:** 5 minutes
Servings: 4

Ingredients:
- 2 green tomatoes, sliced
- Salt and black pepper to the taste
- ½ cup flour
- 1 cup buttermilk
- 1 cup panko bread crumbs
- ½ tablespoon Creole seasoning
- Cooking spray

Directions:

1. Season tomato slices with salt and pepper.
2. Put flour in a bowl, buttermilk in another and panko crumbs and Creole seasoning in a third one.
3. Dredge tomato slices in flour, then in buttermilk and panko bread crumbs, place them in your air fryer's basket greased with cooking spray and cook them at 400 degrees F for 5 minutes.
4. Divide among plates and serve as a side dish.

Enjoy!

Nutrition: calories 124, fat 5, fiber 7, carbs 9, protein 4

Cauliflower Cakes

Preparation time: 10 minutes **Cooking time:** 10 minutes
Servings: 6

Ingredients:
- 3 and ½ cups cauliflower rice
- 2 eggs
- ¼ cup white flour
- ½ cup parmesan, grated
- Salt and black pepper to the taste
- Cooking spray

Directions:
1. In a bowl, mix cauliflower rice with salt and pepper, stir and squeeze excess water.
2. Transfer cauliflower to another bowl, add eggs, salt, pepper, flour and parmesan, stir really well and shape your cakes.
3. Grease your air fryer with cooking spray, heat it up at 400 degrees, add cauliflower cakes and cook them for 10 minutes flipping them halfway.
4. Divide cakes on plates and serve as a side dish.

Enjoy!

Nutrition: calories 125, fat 2, fiber 6, carbs 8, protein 3

Creamy Brussels Sprouts

Preparation time: 10 minutes **Cooking time:** 25 minutes
Servings: 8

Ingredients:

- 3 pounds Brussels sprouts, halved
- A drizzle of olive oil
- 1 pound bacon, chopped
- Salt and black pepper to the taste
- 4 tablespoons butter
- 3 shallots, chopped
- 1 cup milk
- 2 cups heavy cream
- ¼ teaspoon nutmeg, ground
- 3 tablespoons prepared horseradish

Directions:
1. Preheated you air fryer at 370 degrees F, add oil, bacon, salt and pepper and Brussels sprouts and toss.
2. Add butter, shallots, heavy cream, milk, nutmeg and horseradish, toss again and cook for 25 minutes.
3. Divide among plates and serve as a side dish.

Enjoy!

Nutrition: calories 214, fat 5, fiber 8, carbs 12, protein 5

Cheddar Biscuits

Preparation time: 10 minutes **Cooking time:** 20 minutes
Servings: 8

Ingredients:
- 2 and 1/3 cup self-rising flour
- ½ cup butter+ 1 tablespoon, melted
- 2 tablespoons sugar
- ½ cup cheddar cheese, grated
- 1 and 1/3 cup buttermilk
- 1 cup flour

Directions:
1. In a bowl, mix self-rising flour with ½ cup butter, sugar, cheddar cheese and buttermilk and stir until you obtain a dough.
2. Spread 1 cup flour on a working surface, roll dough, flatten it, cut 8 circles with a cookie cutter and coat them with flour.
3. Line your air fryer's basket with tin foil, add biscuits, brush them with melted butter and cook them at 380 degrees F for 20 minutes.
4. Divide among plates and serve as a side.

Enjoy!

Nutrition: calories 221, fat 3, fiber 8, carbs 12, protein 4

Zucchini Fries

Preparation time: 10 minutes **Cooking time:** 12 minutes
Servings: 4

Ingredients:

- 1 zucchini, cut into medium sticks
- A drizzle of olive oil
- Salt and black pepper to the taste
- 2 eggs, whisked
- 1 cup bread crumbs
- ½ cup flour

Directions:

1. Put flour in a bowl and mix with salt and pepper and stir.
2. Put breadcrumbs in another bowl.
3. In a third bowl mix eggs with a pinch of salt and pepper.
4. Dredge zucchini fries in flour, then in eggs and in bread crumbs at the end.

5. Grease your air fryer with some olive oil, heat up at 400 degrees F, add zucchini fries and cook them for 12 minutes.
6. Serve them as a side dish.

Enjoy!

Nutrition: calories 172, fat 3, fiber 3, carbs 7, protein 3

Roasted Peppers

Preparation time: 10 minutes **Cooking time:** 20 minutes
Servings: 4

Ingredients:

- 1 tablespoon sweet paprika
- 1 tablespoon olive oil
- 4 red bell peppers, cut into medium strips
- 4 green bell peppers, cut into medium strips
- 4 yellow bell peppers, cut into medium strips
- 1 yellow onion, chopped
- Salt and black pepper to the taste

Directions:
1. In your air fryer, mix red bell peppers with green and yellow ones.
2. Add paprika, oil, onion, salt and pepper, toss and cook at 350 degrees F for 20 minutes.
3. Divide among plates and serve as a side dish.

Enjoy!

Nutrition: calories 142, fat 4, fiber 4, carbs 7, protein 4

Creamy Endives

Preparation time: 10 minutes **Cooking time:** 10 minutes
Servings: 6

Ingredients:

- 6 endives, trimmed and halved
- 1 teaspoon garlic powder
- ½ cup Greek yogurt
- ½ teaspoon curry powder
- Salt and black pepper to the taste
- 3 tablespoons lemon juice

Directions:
1. In a bowl, mix endives with garlic powder, yogurt, curry powder, salt, pepper and lemon juice, toss, leave aside for 10 minutes and transfer to your preheated air fryer at 350 degrees F.
2. Cook endives for 10 minutes, divide them on plates and serve as a side dish.

Enjoy!

Nutrition: calories 100, fat 2, fiber 2, carbs 7, protein 4

Delicious Roasted Carrots

Preparation time: 10 minutes **Cooking time:** 20 minutes
Servings: 4

Ingredients:

- 1 pound baby carrots
- 2 teaspoons olive oil
- 1 teaspoon herbs de Provence
- 4 tablespoons orange juice

Directions:

1. In your air fryer's basket, mix carrots with herbs de Provence, oil and orange juice, toss and cook at 320 degrees F for 20 minutes.
2. Divide among plates and serve as a side dish.

Enjoy!

Nutrition: calories 112, fat 2, fiber 3, carbs 4, protein 3

Vermouth Mushrooms

Preparation time: 10 minutes **Cooking time:** 25 minutes
Servings: 4

Ingredients:

- 1 tablespoon olive oil
- 2 pounds white mushrooms
- 2 tablespoons white vermouth
- 2 teaspoons herbs de Provence
- 2 garlic cloves, minced

Directions:

1. In your air fryer, mix oil with mushrooms, herbs de Provence and garlic, toss and cook at 350 degrees F for 20 minutes.
2. Add vermouth, toss and cook for 5 minutes more.
3. Divide among plates and serve as a side dish.

Enjoy!

Nutrition: calories 121, fat 2, fiber 5, carbs 7, protein 4

Roasted Parsnips

Preparation time: 10 minutes **Cooking time:** 40 minutes
Servings: 6

Ingredients:

- 2 pounds parsnips, peeled and cut into medium chunks
- 2 tablespoons maple syrup
- 1 tablespoon parsley flakes, dried
- 1 tablespoon olive oil

Directions:

1. Preheat your air fryer at 360 degrees F, add oil and heat it up as well.
2. Add parsnips, parsley flakes and maple syrup, toss and cook them for 40 minutes.
3. Divide among plates and serve as a side dish.

Enjoy!

Nutrition: calories 124, fat 3, fiber 3, carbs 7, protein 4

Barley Risotto

Preparation time: 10 minutes **Cooking time:** 30 minutes
Servings: 8

Ingredients:

- 5 cups veggie stock
- 3 tablespoons olive oil
- 2 yellow onions, chopped
- 2 garlic cloves, minced
- ¾ pound barley
- 3 ounces mushrooms, sliced
- 2 ounces skim milk
- 1 teaspoon thyme, dried
- 1 teaspoon tarragon, dried
- Salt and black pepper to the taste
- 2 pounds sweet potato, peeled and chopped

Directions:

1. Put stock in a pot, add barley, stir, bring to a boil over medium heat and cook for 15 minutes.
2. Heat up your air fryer at 350 degrees F, add oil and heat it up.

3. Add barley, onions, garlic, mushrooms, milk, salt, pepper, tarragon and sweet potato, stir and cook for 15 minutes more.
4. Divide among plates and serve as a side dish.

Enjoy!

Nutrition: calories 124, fat 4, fiber 4, carbs 6, protein 4

Glazed Beets

Preparation time: 10 minutes **Cooking time:** 40 minutes

Servings: 8

Ingredients:

- 3 pounds small beets, trimmed
- 4 tablespoons maple syrup
- 1 tablespoon duck fat

Directions:

1. Heat up your air fryer at 360 degrees F, add duck fat and heat it up.
2. Add beets and maple syrup, toss and cook for 40 minutes.
3. Divide among plates and serve as a side dish.

Enjoy!

Nutrition: calories 121, fat 3, fiber 2, carbs 3, protein 4

Beer Risotto

Preparation time: 10 minutes **Cooking time:** 30 minutes
Servings: 4

Ingredients:
- 2 tablespoons olive oil
- 2 yellow onions, chopped
- 1 cup mushrooms, sliced
- 1 teaspoon basil, dried
- 1 teaspoon oregano, dried
- 1 and ½ cups rice
- 2 cups beer
- 2 cups chicken stock
- 1 tablespoon butter
- ½ cup parmesan, grated

Directions:
1. In a dish that fits your air fryer, mix oil with onions, mushrooms, basil and oregano and stir.
2. Add rice, beer, butter, stock and butter, stir again, place in your air fryer's basket and cook at 350 degrees F for 30 minutes.
3. Divide among plates and serve with grated parmesan on top as a side dish.

Enjoy!

Nutrition: calories 142, fat 4, fiber 4, carbs 6, protein 4

Cauliflower Rice

Preparation time: 10 minutes **Cooking time:** 40 minutes
Servings: 8

Ingredients:

- 1 tablespoon peanut oil
- 1 tablespoon sesame oil
- 4 tablespoons soy sauce
- 3 garlic cloves, minced
- 1 tablespoon ginger, grated
- Juice from ½ lemon
- 1 cauliflower head, riced
- 9 ounces water chestnuts, drained
- ¾ cup peas
- 15 ounces mushrooms, chopped
- 1 egg, whisked

Directions:
1. In your air fryer, mix cauliflower rice with peanut oil, sesame oil, soy sauce, garlic, ginger and lemon juice, stir, cover and cook at 350 degrees F for 20 minutes.
2. Add chestnuts, peas, mushrooms and egg, toss and cook at 360 degrees F for 20 minutes more.
3. Divide among plates and serve for breakfast.

Enjoy!

Nutrition: calories 142, fat 3, fiber 2, carbs 6, protein 4

Carrots and Rhubarb

Preparation time: 10 minutes **Cooking time:** 40 minutes
Servings: 4

Ingredients:
- 1 pound baby carrots
- 2 teaspoons walnut oil
- 1 pound rhubarb, roughly chopped
- 1 orange, peeled, cut into medium segments and zest grated
- ½ cup walnuts, halved
- ½ teaspoon stevia

Directions:
1. Put the oil in your air fryer, add carrots, toss and fry them at 380 degrees F for 20 minutes.
2. Add rhubarb, orange zest, stevia and walnuts, toss and cook for 20 minutes more.
3. Add orange segments, toss and serve as a side dish.

Enjoy!

Nutrition: calories 172, fat 2, fiber 3, carbs 4, protein 4

Roasted Eggplant

Preparation time: 10 minutes **Cooking time:** 20 minutes
Servings: 6

Ingredients:

- 1 and ½ pounds eggplant, cubed
- 1 tablespoon olive oil
- 1 teaspoon garlic powder
- 1 teaspoon onion powder
- 1 teaspoon sumac
- 2 teaspoons za'atar
- Juice from ½ lemon
- 2 bay leaves

Directions:

1. In your air fryer, mix eggplant cubes with oil, garlic powder, onion powder, sumac, za'atar, lemon juice and bay leaves, toss and cook at 370 degrees F for 20 minutes.
2. Divide among plates and serve as a side dish.

Enjoy!

Nutrition: calories 172, fat 4, fiber 7, carbs 12, protein 3

Delicious Air Fried Broccoli

Preparation time: 10 minutes **Cooking time:** 20 minutes
Servings: 4

Ingredients:

- 1 tablespoon duck fat
- 1 broccoli head, florets separated
- 3 garlic cloves, minced
- Juice from ½ lemon
- 1 tablespoon sesame seeds

Directions:

1. Heat up your air fryer at 350 degrees F, add duck fat and heat as well.
2. Add broccoli, garlic, lemon juice and sesame seeds, toss and cook for 20 minutes.
3. Divide among plates and serve as a side dish.

Enjoy!

Nutrition: calories 132, fat 3, fiber 3, carbs 6, protein 4

Onion Rings Side Dish

Preparation time: 10 minutes **Cooking time:** 10 minutes
Servings: 3

Ingredients:

- 1 onion cut into medium slices and rings separated
- 1 and ¼ cups white flour
- A pinch of salt
- 1 egg
- 1 cup milk
- 1 teaspoon baking powder
- ¾ cup bread crumbs

Directions:
1. In a bowl, mix flour with salt and baking powder, stir, dredge onion rings in this mix and place them on a separate plate.
2. Add milk and egg to flour mix and whisk well.
3. Dip onion rings in this mix, dredge them in breadcrumbs, put them in your air fryer's basket and cook them at 360 degrees F for 10 minutes.
4. Divide among plates and serve as a side dish for a steak.

Enjoy!

Nutrition: calories 140, fat 8, fiber 20, carbs 12, protein 3

Rice and Sausage Side Dish

Preparation time: 10 minutes **Cooking time:** 20 minutes
Servings: 4

Ingredients:
- 2 cups white rice, already boiled
- 1 tablespoon butter
- Salt and black pepper to the taste
- 4 garlic cloves, minced
- 1 pork sausage, chopped
- 2 tablespoons carrot, chopped
- 3 tablespoons cheddar cheese, grated
- 2 tablespoons mozzarella cheese, shredded

Directions:
1. Heat up your air fryer at 350 degrees F, add butter, melt it, add garlic, stir and brown for 2 minutes.
2. Add sausage, salt, pepper, carrots and rice, stir and cook at 350 degrees F for 10 minutes.
3. Add cheddar and mozzarella, toss, divide among plates and serve as a side dish.

Enjoy!

Nutrition: calories 240, fat 12, fiber 5, carbs 20, protein 13

Banana Chips

Preparation time: 10 minutes **Cooking time:** 15 minutes

Servings: 4

Ingredients:

- 4 bananas, peeled and sliced
- A pinch of salt
- ½ teaspoon turmeric powder
- ½ teaspoon chaat masala
- 1 teaspoon olive oil

Directions:

1. In a bowl, mix banana slices with salt, turmeric, chaat masala and oil, toss and leave aside for 10 minutes.
2. Transfer banana slices to your preheated air fryer at 360 degrees F and cook them for 15 minutes flipping them once.
3. Serve as a snack.

Enjoy!

Nutrition: calories 121, fat 1, fiber 2, carbs 3, protein 3

Spring Rolls

Preparation time: 10 minutes **Cooking time:** 25 minutes
Servings: 8

Ingredients:

- 2 cups green cabbage, shredded
- 2 yellow onions, chopped
- 1 carrot, grated
- ½ chili pepper, minced
- 1 tablespoon ginger, grated
- 3 garlic cloves, minced
- 1 teaspoon sugar
- Salt and black pepper to the taste
- 1 teaspoon soy sauce
- 2 tablespoons olive oil
- 10 spring roll sheets
- 2 tablespoons corn flour
- 2 tablespoons water

Directions:

1. Heat up a pan with the oil over medium heat, add cabbage, onions, carrots, chili pepper, ginger, garlic,

sugar, salt, pepper and soy sauce, stir well, cook for 2-3 minutes, take off heat and cool down.
2. Cut spring roll sheets in squares, divide cabbage mix on each and roll them.
3. In a bowl, mix corn flour with water, stir well and seal spring rolls with this mix.
4. Place spring rolls in your air fryer's basket and cook them at 360 degrees F for 10 minutes.
5. Flip roll and cook them for 10 minutes more.
6. Arrange on a platter and serve them as an appetizer.

Enjoy!

Nutrition: calories 214, fat 4, fiber 4, carbs 12, protein 4

Crispy Radish Chips

Preparation time: 10 minutes **Cooking time:** 10 minutes
Servings: 4

Ingredients:

- Cooking spray
- 15 radishes, sliced
- Salt and black pepper to the taste
- 1 tablespoon chives, chopped

Directions:

1. Arrange radish slices in your air fryer's basket, spray them with cooking oil, season with salt and black pepper to the taste, cook them at 350 degrees F for 10 minutes, flipping them halfway, transfer to bowls and serve with chives sprinkled on top.

Enjoy!

Nutrition: calories 80, fat 1, fiber 1, carbs 1, protein 1

Crab Sticks

Preparation time: 10 minutes **Cooking time:** 12 minutes
Servings: 4

Ingredients:

- 10 crabsticks, halved
- 2 teaspoons sesame oil
- 2 teaspoons Cajun seasoning

Directions:

1. Put crab sticks in a bowl, add sesame oil and Cajun seasoning, toss, transfer them to your air fryer's basket and cook at 350 degrees F for 12 minutes. Arrange on a platter and serve as an appetizer.

Enjoy!

Nutrition: calories 110, fat 0, fiber 1, carbs 4, protein 2

Air Fried Dill Pickles

Preparation time: 10 minutes **Cooking time:** 5 minutes
Servings: 4

Ingredients:

- 16 ounces jarred dill pickles, cut into wedges and pat dried
- ½ cup white flour
- 1 egg
- ¼ cup milk
- ½ teaspoon garlic powder
- ½ teaspoon sweet paprika
- Cooking spray
- ¼ cup ranch sauce

Directions:

1. In a bowl, combine milk with egg and whisk well.
2. In a second bowl, mix flour with salt, garlic powder and paprika and stir as well
3. Dip pickles in flour, then in egg mix and again in flour and place them in your air fryer.

4. Grease them with cooking spray, cook pickle wedges at 400 degrees F for 5 minutes, transfer to a bowl and serve with ranch sauce on the side.

Enjoy!

Nutrition: calories 109, fat 2, fiber 2, carbs 10, protein 4

Chickpeas Snack

Preparation time: 10 minutes **Cooking time:** 10 minutes
Servings: 4

Ingredients:

- 15 ounces canned chickpeas, drained
- ½ teaspoon cumin, ground
- 1 tablespoon olive oil
- 1 teaspoon smoked paprika
- Salt and black pepper to the taste

Directions:

1. In a bowl, mix chickpeas with oil, cumin, paprika, salt and pepper, toss to coat, place them in your fryer's basket and cook at 390 degrees F for 10 minutes.
2. Divide into bowls and serve as a snack.

Enjoy!

Nutrition: calories 140, fat 1, fiber 6, carbs 20, protein 6

Sausage Balls

Preparation time: 10 minutes **Cooking time:** 15 minutes
Servings: 9

Ingredients:

- 4 ounces sausage meat, ground
- Salt and black pepper to the taste
- 1 teaspoon sage
- ½ teaspoon garlic, minced
- 1 small onion, chopped
- 3 tablespoons breadcrumbs

Directions:

1. In a bowl, mix sausage with salt, pepper, sage, garlic, onion and breadcrumbs, stir well and shape small balls out of this mix.
2. Put them in your air fryer's basket, cook at 360 degrees F for 15 minutes, divide into bowls and serve as a snack.

Enjoy!

Nutrition: calories 130, fat 7, fiber 1, carbs 13, protein 4

Chicken Dip

Preparation time: 10 minutes **Cooking time:** 25 minutes
Servings: 10

Ingredients:

- 3 tablespoons butter, melted
- 1 cup yogurt
- 12 ounces cream cheese
- 2 cups chicken meat, cooked and shredded
- 2 teaspoons curry powder
- 4 scallions, chopped
- 6 ounces Monterey jack cheese, grated
- 1/3 cup raisins
- ¼ cup cilantro, chopped
- ½ cup almonds, sliced
- Salt and black pepper to the taste
- ½ cup chutney

Directions:

1. In a bowl mix cream cheese with yogurt and whisk using your mixer.

2. Add curry powder, scallions, chicken meat, raisins, cheese, cilantro, salt and pepper and stir everything.
3. Spread this into a baking dish that fist your air fryer, sprinkle almonds on top, place in your air fryer, bake at 300 degrees for 25 minutes, divide into bowls, top with chutney and serve as an appetizer.

Enjoy!

Nutrition: calories 240, fat 10, fiber 2, carbs 24, protein 12

Sweet Popcorn

Preparation time: 5 minutes **Cooking time:** 10 minutes
Servings: 4

Ingredients:
- 2 tablespoons corn kernels
- 2 and ½ tablespoons butter
- 2 ounces brown sugar

Directions:
1. Put corn kernels in your air fryer's pan, cook at 400 degrees F for 6 minutes, transfer them to a tray, spread and leave aside for now.
2. Heat up a pan over low heat, add butter, melt it, add sugar and stir until it dissolves.
3. Add popcorn, toss to coat, take off heat and spread on the tray again.
4. Cool down, divide into bowls and serve as a snack. Enjoy!

Nutrition: calories 70, fat 0.2, fiber 0, carbs 1, protein 1

Apple Chips

Preparation time: 10 minutes **Cooking time:** 10 minutes
Servings: 2

Ingredients:

- 1 apple, cored and sliced
- A pinch of salt
- ½ teaspoon cinnamon powder
- 1 tablespoon white sugar

Directions:

1. In a bowl, mix apple slices with salt, sugar and cinnamon, toss, transfer to your air fryer's basket, cook for 10 minutes at 390 degrees F flipping once.
2. Divide apple chips in bowls and serve as a snack.

Enjoy!

Nutrition: calories 70, fat 0, fiber 4, carbs 3, protein 1

Bread Sticks

Preparation time: 10 minutes **Cooking time:** 10 minutes
Servings: 2

Ingredients:

- 4 bread slices, each cut into 4 sticks
- 2 eggs
- ¼ cup milk
- 1 teaspoon cinnamon powder
- 1 tablespoon honey
- ¼ cup brown sugar
- A pinch of nutmeg

Directions:

1. In a bowl, mix eggs with milk, brown sugar, cinnamon, nutmeg and honey and whisk well.
2. Dip bread sticks in this mix, place them in your air fryer's basket and cook at 360 degrees F for 10 minutes.
3. Divide bread sticks into bowls and serve as a snack.

Enjoy!

Nutrition: calories 140, fat 1, fiber 4, carbs 8, protein 4

Crispy Shrimp

Preparation time: 10 minutes **Cooking time:** 5 minutes
Servings: 4

Ingredients:
- 12 big shrimp, deveined and peeled
- 2 egg whites
- 1 cup coconut, shredded
- 1 cup panko bread crumbs
- 1 cup white flour
- Salt and black pepper to the taste

Directions:
1. In a bowl, mix panko with coconut and stir.
2. Put flour, salt and pepper in a second bowl and whisk egg whites in a third one.
3. Dip shrimp in flour, egg whites mix and coconut, place them all in your air fryer's basket, cook at 350 degrees F for 10 minutes flipping halfway.
4. Arrange on a platter and serve as an appetizer.

Enjoy!

Nutrition: calories 140, fat 4, fiber 0, carbs 3, protein 4

Cajun Shrimp Appetizer

Preparation time: 10 minutes **Cooking time:** 5 minutes
Servings: 2

Ingredients:

- 20 tiger shrimp, peeled and deveined
- Salt and black pepper to the taste
- ½ teaspoon old bay seasoning
- 1 tablespoon olive oil
- ¼ teaspoon smoked paprika

Directions:

1. In a bowl, mix shrimp with oil, salt, pepper, old bay seasoning and paprika and toss to coat.
2. Place shrimp in your air fryer's basket and cook at 390 degrees F for 5 minutes.
3. Arrange them on a platter and serve as an appetizer.

Enjoy!

Nutrition: calories 162, fat 6, fiber 4, carbs 8, protein 14

Crispy Fish Sticks

Preparation time: 10 minutes **Cooking time:** 12 minutes
Servings: 2

Ingredients:

- 4 ounces bread crumbs
- 4 tablespoons olive oil
- 1 egg, whisked
- 4 white fish filets, boneless, skinless and cut into medium sticks
- Salt and black pepper to the taste

Directions:
1. In a bowl, mix bread crumbs with oil and stir well.
2. Put egg in a second bowl, add salt and pepper and whisk well.
3. Dip fish stick in egg and them in bread crumb mix, place them in your air fryer's basket and cook at 360 degrees F for 12 minutes.
4. Arrange fish sticks on a platter and serve as an appetizer.

Enjoy!

Nutrition: calories 160, fat 3, fiber 5, carbs 12, protein 3

Fish Nuggets

Preparation time: 10 minutes **Cooking time:** 12 minutes **Servings:** 4

Ingredients:
- 28 ounces fish fillets, skinless and cut into medium pieces
- Salt and black pepper to the taste
- 5 tablespoons flour
- 1 egg, whisked
- 5 tablespoons water
- 3 ounces panko bread crumbs
- 1 tablespoon garlic powder
- 1 tablespoon smoked paprika
- 4 tablespoons homemade mayonnaise
- Lemon juice from ½ lemon
- 1 teaspoon dill, dried
- Cooking spray

Directions:
1. In a bowl, mix flour with water and stir well.
2. Add egg, salt and pepper and whisk well.

3. In a second bowl, mix panko with garlic powder and paprika and stir well.
4. Dip fish pieces in flour and egg mix and then in panko mix, place them in your air fryer's basket, spray them with cooking oil and cook at 400 degrees F for 12 minutes.
5. Meanwhile, in a bowl mix mayo with dill and lemon juice and whisk well.
6. Arrange fish nuggets on a platter and serve with dill mayo on the side.

Enjoy!

Nutrition: calories 332, fat 12, fiber 6, carbs 17, protein 15

Shrimp and Chestnut Rolls

Preparation time: 10 minutes **Cooking time:** 15 minutes
Servings: 4

Ingredients:

- ½ pound already cooked shrimp, chopped
- 8 ounces water chestnuts, chopped
- ½ pounds shiitake mushrooms, chopped
- 2 cups cabbage, chopped
- 2 tablespoons olive oil
- 1 garlic clove, minced
- 1 teaspoon ginger, grated
- 3 scallions, chopped
- Salt and black pepper to the taste
- 1 tablespoon water
- 1 egg yolk
- 6 spring roll wrappers

Directions:

1. Heat up a pan with the oil over medium high heat, add cabbage, shrimp, chestnuts, mushrooms, garlic, ginger, scallions, salt and pepper, stir and cook for 2 minutes.

2. In a bowl, mix egg with water and stir well.
3. Arrange roll wrappers on a working surface, divide shrimp and veggie mix on them, seal edges with egg wash, place them all in your air fryer's basket, cook at 360 degrees F for 15 minutes, transfer to a platter and serve as an appetizer.

Enjoy!

Nutrition: calories 140, fat 3, fiber 1, carbs 12, protein 3

Seafood Appetizer

Preparation time: 10 minutes **Cooking time:** 25 minutes
Servings: 4

Ingredients:

- ½ cup yellow onion, chopped
- 1 cup green bell pepper, chopped
- 1 cup celery, chopped
- 1 cup baby shrimp, peeled and deveined
- 1 cup crabmeat, flaked
- 1 cup homemade mayonnaise
- 1 teaspoon Worcestershire sauce
- Salt and black pepper to the taste
- 2 tablespoons bread crumbs
- 1 tablespoon butter
- 1 teaspoon sweet paprika

Directions:

1. In a bowl, mix shrimp with crab meat, bell pepper, onion, mayo, celery, salt and pepper and stir.
2. Add Worcestershire sauce, stir again and pour everything into a baking dish that fits your air fryer.

3. Sprinkle bread crumbs and add butter, introduce in your air fryer and cook at 320 degrees F for 25 minutes, shaking halfway.
4. Divide into bowl and serve with paprika sprinkled on top as an appetizer.

Enjoy!

Nutrition: calories 200, fat 1, fiber 2, carbs 5, protein 1

Salmon Meatballs

Preparation time: 10 minutes **Cooking time:** 12 minutes
Servings: 4

Ingredients:

- 3 tablespoons cilantro, minced
- 1 pound salmon, skinless and chopped
- 1 small yellow onion, chopped
- 1 egg white
- Salt and black pepper to the taste
- 2 garlic cloves, minced
- ½ teaspoon paprika
- ¼ cup panko
- ½ teaspoon oregano, ground
- Cooking spray

Directions:

1. In your food processor, mix salmon with onion, cilantro, egg white, garlic cloves, salt, pepper, paprika and oregano and stir well.
2. Add panko, blend again and shape meatballs from this mix using your palms.

3. Place them in your air fryer's basket, spray them with cooking spray and cook at 320 degrees F for 12 minutes shaking the fryer halfway.
4. Arrange meatballs on a platter and serve them as an appetizer.

Enjoy!

Nutrition: calories 289, fat 12, fiber 3, carbs 22, protein 23

Easy Chicken Wings

Preparation time: 10 minutes **Cooking time:** 1 hours **Servings:** 2

Ingredients:

- 16 pieces chicken wings
- Salt and black pepper to the taste
- ¼ cup butter
- ¾ cup potato starch
- ¼ cup honey
- 4 tablespoons garlic, minced

Directions:
1. In a bowl, mix chicken wings with salt, pepper and potato starch, toss well, transfer to your air fryer's basket, cook them at 380 degrees F for 25 minutes and at 400 degrees F for 5 minutes more.
2. Meanwhile, heat up a pan with the butter over medium high heat, melt it, add garlic, stir, cook for 5 minutes and then mix with salt, pepper and honey.
3. Whisk well, cook over medium heat for 20 minutes and take off heat.
4. Arrange chicken wings on a platter, drizzle honey sauce all over and serve as an appetizer.

Enjoy!

Nutrition: calories 244, fat 7, fiber 3, carbs 19, protein 8

Chicken Breast Rolls

Preparation time: 10 minutes **Cooking time:** 22 minutes
Servings: 4

Ingredients:

- 2 cups baby spinach
- 4 chicken breasts, boneless and skinless
- 1 cup sun dried tomatoes, chopped
- Salt and black pepper to the taste
- 1 and ½ tablespoons Italian seasoning
- 4 mozzarella slices
- A drizzle of olive oil

Directions:
1. Flatten chicken breasts using a meat tenderizer, divide tomatoes, mozzarella and spinach, season with salt, pepper and Italian seasoning, roll and seal them.
2. Place them in your air fryer's basket, drizzle some oil over them and cook at 375 degrees F for 17 minutes, flipping once.
3. Arrange chicken rolls on a platter and serve them as an appetizer.

Enjoy!

Nutrition: calories 300, fat 1, fiber 4, carbs 7, protein 10

Crispy Chicken Breast Sticks

Preparation time: 10 minutes **Cooking time:** 16 minutes **Servings:** 4

Ingredients:

- ¾ cup white flour
- 1 pound chicken breast, skinless, boneless and cut into medium sticks
- 1 teaspoon sweet paprika
- 1 cup panko bread crumbs
- 1 egg, whisked
- Salt and black pepper to the taste
- ½ tablespoon olive oil
- Zest from 1 lemon, grated

Directions:
1. In a bowl, mix paprika with flour, salt, pepper and lemon zest and stir.
2. Put whisked egg in another bowl and the panko breadcrumbs in a third one.
3. Dredge chicken pieces in flour, egg and panko and place them in your lined air fryer's basket, drizzle the oil over them, cook at 400 degrees F for 8 minutes, flip and cook for 8 more minutes.
4. Arrange them on a platter and serve as a snack.

Enjoy!

Nutrition: calories 254, fat 4, fiber 7, carbs 20, protein 22

Beef Roll s

Preparation time: 10 minutes **Cooking time:** 14 minutes
Servings: 4

Ingredients:
- 2 pounds beef steak, opened and flattened with a meat tenderizer
- Salt and black pepper to the taste
- 1 cup baby spinach
- 3 ounces red bell pepper, roasted and chopped
- 6 slices provolone cheese
- 3 tablespoons pesto

Directions:
1. Arrange flattened beef steak on a cutting board, spread pesto all over, add cheese in a single layer, add bell peppers, spinach, salt and pepper to the taste.
2. Roll your steak, secure with toothpicks, season again with salt and pepper, place roll in your air fryer's basket and cook at 400 degrees F for 14 minutes, rotating roll halfway.
3. Leave aside to cool down, cut into 2 inch smaller rolls, arrange on a platter and serve them as an appetizer.

Enjoy!

Nutrition: calories 230, fat 1, fiber 3, carbs 12, protein 10

Empanadas

Preparation time: 10 minutes **Cooking time:** 25 minutes
Servings: 4

Ingredients:

- 1 package empanada shells
- 1 tablespoon olive oil
- 1 pound beef meat, ground
- 1 yellow onion, chopped
- Salt and black pepper to the taste
- 2 garlic cloves, minced
- ½ teaspoon cumin, ground
- ¼ cup tomato salsa
- 1 egg yolk whisked with 1 tablespoon water
- 1 green bell pepper, chopped

Directions:

1. Heat up a pan with the oil over medium high heat, add beef and brown on all sides.
2. Add onion, garlic, salt, pepper, bell pepper and tomato salsa, stir and cook for 15 minutes.

3. Divide cooked meat in empanada shells, brush them with egg wash and seal.
4. Place them in your air fryer's steamer basket and cook at 350 degrees F for 10 minutes.
5. Arrange on a platter and serve as an appetizer.

Enjoy!

Nutrition: calories 274, fat 17, fiber 14, carbs 20, protein 7

Greek Lamb Meatballs

Preparation time: 10 minutes **Cooking time:** 8 minutes
Servings: 10

Ingredients:

- 4 ounces lamb meat, minced
- Salt and black pepper to the taste
- 1 slice of bread, toasted and crumbled
- 2 tablespoons feta cheese, crumbled
- ½ tablespoon lemon peel, grated
- 1 tablespoon oregano, chopped

Directions:

1. In a bowl, combine meat with bread crumbs, salt, pepper, feta, oregano and lemon peel, stir well, shape 10 meatballs and place them in you air fryer.
2. Cook at 400 degrees F for 8 minutes, arrange them on a platter and serve as an appetizer.

Enjoy!

Nutrition: calories 234, fat 12, fiber 2, carbs 20, protein 30

Beef Party Rolls

Preparation time: 10 minutes **Cooking time:** 15 minutes
Servings: 4

Ingredients:

- 14 ounces beef stock
- 7 ounces white wine
- 4 beef cutlets
- Salt and black pepper to the taste
- 8 sage leaves
- 4 ham slices
- 1 tablespoon butter, melted

Directions:

1. Heat up a pan with the stock over medium high heat, add wine, cook until it reduces, take off heat and divide into small bowls
2. Season cutlets with salt and pepper, cover with sage and roll each in ham slices.
3. Brush rolls with butter, place them in your air fryer's basket and cook at 400 degrees F for 15 minutes.

4. Arrange rolls on a platter and serve them with the gravy on the side.

Enjoy!

Nutrition: calories 260, fat 12, fiber 1, carbs 22, protein 21

Pork Rolls

Preparation time: 10 minutes **Cooking time:** 40 minutes
Servings: 4

Ingredients:

- 1 15 ounces pork fillet
- ½ teaspoon chili powder
- 1 teaspoon cinnamon powder
- 1 garlic clove, minced
- Salt and black pepper to the taste
- 2 tablespoons olive oil
- 1 and ½ teaspoon cumin, ground
- 1 red onion, chopped
- 3 tablespoons parsley, chopped

Directions:

1. In a bowl, mix cinnamon with garlic, salt, pepper, chili powder, oil, onion, parsley and cumin and stir well
2. Put pork fillet on a cutting board, flatten it using a meat tenderizer. And use a meat tenderizer to flatten it.

3. Spread onion mix on pork, roll tight, cut into medium rolls, place them in your preheated air fryer at 360 degrees F and cook them for 35 minutes.
4. Arrange them on a platter and serve as an appetizer

Enjoy!

Nutrition: calories 304, fat 12, fiber 1, carbs 15, protein 23

Beef Patties

Preparation time: 10 minutes **Cooking time:** 8 minutes
Servings: 4

Ingredients:
- 14 ounces beef, minced
- 2 tablespoons ham, cut into strips
- 1 leek, chopped
- 3 tablespoons bread crumbs
- Salt and black pepper to the taste
- ½ teaspoon nutmeg, ground

Directions:
1. In a bowl, mix beef with leek, salt, pepper, ham, breadcrumbs and nutmeg, stir well and shape small patties out of this mix.
2. Place them in your air fryer's basket, cook at 400 degrees F for 8 minutes, arrange on a platter and serve as an appetizer.

Enjoy!

Nutrition: calories 260, fat 12, fiber 3, carbs 12, protein 21

Roasted Bell Pepper Rolls

Preparation time: 10 minutes **Cooking time:** 10 minutes **Servings:** 8

Ingredients:
- 1 yellow bell pepper, halved
- 1 orange bell pepper, halved
- Salt and black pepper to the taste
- 4 ounces feta cheese, crumbled
- 1 green onion, chopped
- 2 tablespoons oregano, chopped

Directions:
1. In a bowl, mix cheese with onion, oregano, salt and pepper and whisk well.
2. Place bell pepper halves in your air fryer's basket, cook at 400 degrees F for 10 minutes, transfer to a cutting board, cool down and peel.
3. Divide cheese mix on each bell pepper half, roll, secure with toothpicks, arrange on a platter and serve as an appetizer.

Enjoy!

Nutrition: calories 170, fat 1, fiber 2, carbs 8, protein 5

Stuffed Peppers

Preparation time: 10 minutes **Cooking time:** 8 minutes
Servings: 8

Ingredients:

- 8 small bell peppers, tops cut off and seeds removed
- 1 tablespoon olive oil
- Salt and black pepper to the taste
- 3.5 ounces goat cheese, cut into 8 pieces

Directions:

1. In a bowl, mix cheese with oil with salt and pepper and toss to coat.
2. Stuff each pepper with goat cheese, place them in your air fryer's basket, cook at 400 degrees F for 8 minutes, arrange on a platter and serve as an appetizer.

Enjoy!

Nutrition: calories 120, fat 1, fiber 1, carbs 12, protein 8

Herbed Tomatoes Appetizer

Preparation time: 10 minutes **Cooking time:** 20 minutes
Servings: 2

Ingredients:
- 2 tomatoes, halved
- Cooking spray
- Salt and black pepper to the taste
- 1 teaspoon parsley, dried
- 1 teaspoon basil, dried
- 1 teaspoon oregano, dried
- 1 teaspoon rosemary, dried

Directions:
1. Spray tomato halves with cooking oil, season with salt, pepper, parsley, basil, oregano and rosemary over them.
2. Place them in your air fryer's basket and cook at 320 degrees F for 20 minutes.
3. Arrange them on a platter and serve as an appetizer.

Enjoy!

Nutrition: calories 100, fat 1, fiber 1, carbs 4, protein 1

Olives Balls

Preparation time: 10 minutes **Cooking time:** 4 minutes
Servings: 6

Ingredients:
- 8 black olives, pitted and minced
- Salt and black pepper to the taste
- 2 tablespoons sun dried tomato pesto
- 14 pepperoni slices, chopped
- 4 ounces cream cheese
- 1 tablespoons basil, chopped

Directions:

1. In a bowl, mix cream cheese with salt, pepper, basil, pepperoni, pesto and black olives, stir well and shape small balls out of this mix.
2. Place them in your air fryer's basket, cook at 350 degrees F for 4 minutes, arrange on a platter and serve as a snack.

Enjoy!

Nutrition: calories 100, fat 1, fiber 0, carbs 8, protein 3

Jalapeno Balls

Preparation time: 10 minutes **Cooking time:** 4 minutes **Servings:** 3

Ingredients:
- 3 bacon slices, cooked and crumbled
- 3 ounces cream cheese
- ¼ teaspoon onion powder
- Salt and black pepper to the taste
- 1 jalapeno pepper, chopped
- ½ teaspoon parsley, dried
- ¼ teaspoon garlic powder

Directions:
1. In a bowl, mix cream cheese with jalapeno pepper, onion and garlic powder, parsley, bacon salt and pepper and stir well.
2. Shape small balls out of this mix, place them in your air fryer's basket, cook at 350 degrees F for 4 minutes, arrange on a platter and serve as an appetizer.

Enjoy!

Nutrition: calories 172, fat 4, fiber 1, carbs 12, protein 5

Wrapped Shrimp

Preparation time: 10 minutes **Cooking time:** 8 minutes **Servings:** 16

Ingredients:
- 2 tablespoons olive oil
- 10 ounces already cooked shrimp, peeled and deveined
- 1 tablespoons mint, chopped
- 1/3 cup blackberries, ground
- 11 prosciutto sliced
- 1/3 cup red wine

Directions:

1. Wrap each shrimp in a prosciutto slices, drizzle the oil over them, rub well, place in your preheated air fryer at 390 degrees F and fry them for 8 minutes.
2. Meanwhile, heat up a pan with ground blackberries over medium heat, add mint and wine, stir, cook for 3 minutes and take off heat.
3. Arrange shrimp on a platter, drizzle blackberries sauce over them and serve as an appetizer.

Enjoy!

Nutrition: calories 224, fat 12, fiber 2, carbs 12, protein 14

Broccoli Patties

Preparation time: 10 minutes **Cooking time:** 10 minutes **Servings:** 12

Ingredients:

- 4 cups broccoli florets
- 1 and ½ cup almond flour
- 1 teaspoon paprika
- Salt and black pepper to the taste
- 2 eggs
- ¼ cup olive oil
- 2 cups cheddar cheese, grated
- 1 teaspoon garlic powder
- ½ teaspoon apple cider vinegar
- ½ teaspoon baking soda

Directions:

1. Put broccoli florets in your food processor, add salt and pepper, blend well and transfer to a bowl.
2. Add almond flour, salt, pepper, paprika, garlic powder, baking soda, cheese, oil, eggs and vinegar, stir well and shape 12 patties out of this mix.

3. Place them in your preheated air fryer's basket and cook at 350 degrees F for 10 minutes.
4. Arrange patties on a platter and serve as an appetizer. Enjoy!

Nutrition: calories 203, fat 12, fiber 2, carbs 14, protein 2

Different Stuffed Peppers

Preparation time: 10 minutes **Cooking time:** 20 minutes

Servings: 6

Ingredients:

- 1 pound mini bell peppers, halved
- Salt and black pepper to the taste
- 1 teaspoon garlic powder
- 1 teaspoon sweet paprika
- ½ teaspoon oregano, dried
- ¼ teaspoon red pepper flakes
- 1 pound beef meat, ground
- 1 and ½ cups cheddar cheese, shredded
- 1 tablespoons chili powder
- 1 teaspoon cumin, ground
- Sour cream for serving

Directions:

1. In a bowl, mix chili powder with paprika, salt, pepper, cumin, oregano, pepper flakes and garlic powder and stir.

2. Heat up a pan over medium heat, add beef, stir and brown for 10 minutes.
3. Add chili powder mix, stir, take off heat and stuff pepper halves with this mix.
4. Sprinkle cheese all over, place peppers in your air fryer's basket and cook them at 350 degrees F for 6 minutes.
5. Arrange peppers on a platter and serve them with sour cream on the side.

Enjoy!

Nutrition: calories 170, fat 22, fiber 3, carbs 6, protein 27

Cheesy Zucchini Snack

Preparation time: 10 minutes **Cooking time:** 8 minutes **Servings:** 4

Ingredients:
- 1 cup mozzarella, shredded
- ¼ cup tomato sauce
- 1 zucchini, sliced
- Salt and black pepper to the taste
- A pinch of cumin
- Cooking spray

Directions:

1. Arrange zucchini slices in your air fryer's basket, spray them with cooking oil, spread tomato sauce all over, them, season with salt, pepper, cumin, sprinkle mozzarella at the end and cook them at 320 degrees F for 8 minutes.
2. Arrange them on a platter and serve as a snack.

Enjoy!

Nutrition: calories 150, fat 4, fiber 2, carbs 12, protein 4

Spinach Balls

Preparation time: 10 minutes **Cooking time:** 7 minutes **Servings:** 30

Ingredients:

- 4 tablespoons butter, melted
- 2 eggs
- 1 cup flour
- 16 ounces spinach
- 1/3 cup feta cheese, crumbled
- ¼ teaspoon nutmeg, ground
- 1/3 cup parmesan, grated
- Salt and black pepper to the taste
- 1 tablespoon onion powder
- 3 tablespoons whipping cream
- 1 teaspoon garlic powder

Directions:

1. In your blender, mix spinach with butter, eggs, flour, feta cheese, parmesan, nutmeg, whipping cream, salt, pepper, onion and garlic pepper, blend very well and keep in the freezer for 10 minutes.

2. Shape 30 spinach balls, place them in your air fryer's basket and cook at 300 degrees F for 7 minutes.
3. Serve as a party appetizer.

Enjoy!

Nutrition: calories 60, fat 5, fiber 1, carbs 1, protein 2

Mushrooms Appetizer

Preparation time: 10 minutes **Cooking time:** 10 minutes
Servings: 4

Ingredients:

- ¼ cup mayonnaise
- 1 teaspoon garlic powder
- 1 small yellow onion, chopped
- 24 ounces white mushroom caps
- Salt and black pepper to the taste
- 1 teaspoon curry powder
- 4 ounces cream cheese, soft
- ¼ cup sour cream
- ½ cup Mexican cheese, shredded
- 1 cup shrimp, cooked, peeled, deveined and chopped

Directions:

1. In a bowl, mix mayo with garlic powder, onion, curry powder, cream cheese, sour cream, Mexican cheese, shrimp, salt and pepper to the taste and whisk well.

2. Stuff mushrooms with this mix, place them in your air fryer's basket and cook at 300 degrees F for 10 minutes.
3. Arrange on a platter and serve as an appetizer. Enjoy!

Nutrition: calories 200, fat 20, fiber 3, carbs 16, protein 14

Cheesy Party Wings

Preparation time: 10 minutes **Cooking time:** 12 minutes
Servings: 6

Ingredients:

- 6 pound chicken wings, halved
- Salt and black pepper to the taste
- ½ teaspoon Italian seasoning
- 2 tablespoons butter
- ½ cup parmesan cheese, grated
- A pinch of red pepper flakes, crushed
- 1 teaspoon garlic powder
- 1 egg

Directions:

1. Arrange chicken wings in your air fryer's basket and cook at 390 degrees F and cook for 9 minutes.
2. Meanwhile, in your blender, mix butter with cheese, egg, salt, pepper, pepper flakes, garlic powder and Italian seasoning and blend very well.

3. Take chicken wings out, pour cheese sauce over them, toss to coat well and cook in your air fryer's basket at 390 degrees F for 3 minutes.
4. Serve them as an appetizer.

Enjoy!

Nutrition: calories 204, fat 8, fiber 1, carbs 18, protein 14

Cheese Sticks

Preparation time: 1 hour and 10 minutes **Cooking time:** 8 minutes **Servings:** 16

Ingredients:

- 2 eggs, whisked
- Salt and black pepper to the taste
- 8 mozzarella cheese strings, cut into halves
- 1 cup parmesan, grated
- 1 tablespoon Italian seasoning
- Cooking spray
- 1 garlic clove, minced

Directions:

1. In a bowl, mix parmesan with salt, pepper, Italian seasoning and garlic and stir well.
2. Put whisked eggs in another bowl.
3. Dip mozzarella sticks in egg mixture, then in cheese mix.
4. Dip them again in egg and in parmesan mix and keep them in the freezer for 1 hour.

5. Spray cheese sticks with cooking oil, place them in your air fryer's basket and cook at 390 degrees F for 8 minutes flipping them halfway.
6. Arrange them on a platter and serve as an appetizer. Enjoy!

Nutrition: calories 140, fat 5, fiber 1, carbs 3, protein 4

Sweet Bacon Snack

Preparation time: 10 minutes **Cooking time:** 30 minutes **Servings:** 16

Ingredients:
- ½ teaspoon cinnamon powder
- 16 bacon slices
- 1 tablespoon avocado oil
- 3 ounces dark chocolate
- 1 teaspoon maple extract

Directions:
1. Arrange bacon slices in your air fryer's basket, sprinkle cinnamon mix over them and cook them at 300 degrees F for 30 minutes.
2. Heat up a pot with the oil over medium heat, add chocolate and stir until it melts.
3. Add maple extract, stir, take off heat and leave aside to cool down a bit.
4. Take bacon strips out of the oven, leave them to cool down, dip each in chocolate mix, place them on a

parchment paper and leave them to cool down completely.
5. Serve cold as a snack.

Enjoy!

Nutrition: calories 200, fat 4, fiber 5, carbs 12, protein 3

Chicken Rolls

Preparation time: 2 hours and 10 minutes **Cooking time:** 10 minutes **Servings:** 12

Ingredients:

- 4 ounces blue cheese, crumbled
- 2 cups chicken, cooked and chopped
- Salt and black pepper to the taste
- 2 green onions, chopped
- 2 celery stalks, finely chopped
- ½ cup tomato sauce
- 12 egg roll wrappers
- Cooking spray

Directions:

1. In a bowl, mix chicken meat with blue cheese, salt, pepper, green onions, celery and tomato sauce, stir well and keep in the fridge for 2 hours.
2. Place egg wrappers on a working surface, divide chicken mix on them, roll and seal edges.

3. Place rolls in your air fryer's basket, spray them with cooking oil and cook at 350 degrees F for 10 minutes, flipping them halfway.

Enjoy!

Nutrition: calories 220, fat 7, fiber 2, carbs 14, protein 10

Tasty Kale and Celery Crackers

Preparation time: 10 minutes **Cooking time:** 20 minutes
Servings: 6

Ingredients:

- 2 cups flax seed, ground
- 2 cups flax seed, soaked overnight and drained
- 4 bunches kale, chopped
- 1 bunch basil, chopped
- ½ bunch celery, chopped
- 4 garlic cloves, minced
- 1/3 cup olive oil

Directions:
1. In your food processor mix ground flaxseed with celery, kale, basil and garlic and blend well.
2. Add oil and soaked flaxseed and blend again, spread in your air fryer's pan, cut into medium crackers and cook them at 380 degrees F for 20 minutes.
3. Divide into bowls and serve as an appetizer.

Enjoy!

Nutrition: calories 143, fat 1, fiber 2, carbs 8, protein 4

Conclusion

Air frying is one of the most popular cooking methods these days and air fryers have become one of the most amazing tools in the kitchen.
Air fryers help you cook healthy and delicious meals in no time! You don't need to be an expert in the kitchen in order to cook special dishes for you and your loved ones!
You just have to own an air fryer and this great air fryer cookbook!

You will soon make the best dishes ever and you will impress everyone around you with your home cooked meals!
Just trust us! Get your hands on an air fryer and on this useful air fryer recipes collection and start your new cooking experience!
Have fun!

www.ingramcontent.com/pod-product-compliance
Lightning Source LLC
Chambersburg PA
CBHW071819080526
44589CB00012B/852